Parental Leave

Poems for Parents

By

Anne Marie Brown

Acknowledgements

Cover illustration by: Simona Staykova @Colorful_Simone

All Poetry Copyright
© Anne Marie Brown (@BrunchPoet)
ISBN: 978-0-578-31704-5
Printed by: Amazon KDP
www.AMBrownAuthor.com

Dedication

To Malia and Jack – you are my whole world.
To my husband, Matt, I couldn't survive this journey
without you.

To The New Mom

I know that you're in it,
There's no end in sight,
It feels like they need you
All day and all night.

They're tiny & helpless,
You're tired and sore,
You frequently wonder
How you can give more.

But, mama, I promise
This season will end.
Your baby will sleep and
You'll feel whole again.

I know that it sucks now,
And newborns are tough.
You're not failing mama -
You're doing enough.

Contents

Trying

Hope

Sometimes Hope is hard to hold,
When fear or loss have left you cold
And shattered you upon the shore,
'Till battered, you can float no more.

But Hope is there, clutched in your hand,
She tells you "Up! I know you can!"
And so you rise to fight again,
Uncertain if you'll ever win.

Hope's a small, and fragile thing,
But still she beats her fervent wings,
Even deep within the storm,
She tries her best to keep you warm.

So if today, you're low and lost,
And wonder if it's worth the cost,
Remember what comes after rain -
The sun unveils her vivid train.

When all is gone,
Hope will remain.

Miscarriage

The body mends all broken parts,
But what of life lost at its start?

A piece of me has come apart.
My bones can heal,
But will my heart?

Ectopic

The blood ran red,
I couldn't stop it.

My Doctor said
It was ectopic.

Sure, your existence
Still felt new,

But others said
It wasn't true

To use the phrase
That I "lost" you.

What was the right
Way to describe

The pain, the hole
I felt inside?

You joined my world
In two pink lines.

I almost died.
I wasn't fine.

I know you were
Not meant to be...

But still you were
A part of me.

Tomorrow

Tomorrow isn't promised,
But it's still another day,
Another chance to change the world.
In my own tiny way.

Tomorrow will improve, (I hope),
Today was really tough.
My response was far from perfect,
And my actions weren't enough.

Tomorrow is, and ever was,
A chance to start anew,
Though all the trials we saw today,
We may still yet go through.

Today, I may be hurting,
It may seem it has no end.
Today, I may feel all alone,
And jealous of a friend.

Today, things seem impossible,
I feel like giving in,
But tomorrow's sun will always rise,
A new day will begin.

Today, I'll cry, and wipe my eyes,
Today I'll break like glass.
But tomorrow, I will try again.

I know, this too, shall pass.

My Mama Was My House

My Mama was my house,
A tiny egg so small
That stored the DNA of me –
What made me short, or tall.

My Mama was my house,
You could see her belly grow
While I floated in her uterus
Over 10 long months (or so).

My Mama was my house,
We were connected all along,
Through a cord called the "umbilical"
That helped me grow up strong.

My Mama was my house,
When I uttered my first cry
And said "Hello!" to all the world
And opened up my eyes.

My Mama was my house,
And now I'll never feel alone,
Because when I am in her arms
She'll always be my home.

Fourth Trimester

Dear Mama -

I see you.

I see you in the acronyms you've learned by necessity- TTC, HCG, IVF, IUI, FSH, LH, RSV, NICU.

I see you in the tracking of your body temperature, your ovulation, which breast you fed on last, the exact minute your baby latched, the last time he ate/slept/pooped, the ounces you pumped and those last precious few left in the back of your freezer.

I see you in the disappointment, the frustration, the awe, the exhaustion, and the sheer will to stay awake and hold your baby until her breathing becomes heavy against your chest.

I see you.

I see you covered in milk, your breasts aching and alien and begging for relief. I see your oversupply, your lack of supply, your lactation consultant visits, your mastitis, your searches typed over and over looking for an answer - "what is the best formula?" "Will bottles cause nipple confusion?" "Is my baby eating enough?" "Is my baby throwing up too much?"

"Nipple shields, SNS, Slow Flow bottles, forceful let down, tongue tie, mouth tie, milk blister." I see you crying and comparing yourself to other moms who make it seem to so natural to feed their babies.

I see you in your post-partum diaper, giant pads and crappy underwear trying to sit, to stand, to pee.

I see your C section scar, your ectopic pregnancy scar, your episiotomy scar, your stretch marks, your chapped nipples, your body that is no longer your own.

I hear you.

I hear you in the mechanical pumping that heralds every morning, every evening, every 2-3 hours. I hear you asking for the nearest outlet, the most private corner of the restaurant, the storage closet at work that has been designated as the "nursing room."

I hear you.

I hear you calling out the inventory of the diaper bag as you try to leave the house, as if you were in the operating room asking for instruments - "Diapers? Wipes? Toys? Bottles? Solid food? Milk? Burp cloths?" I hear you stressing to leave on time, every time, because there is never enough time.

I hear you calling the doctor to ask if your Braxton-Hicks contractions are reason to be concerned. If that rash means you should bring her in. If that fever, that cough, that red mark, that spotting, that pain is something you should worry about, because you are worried - you are always worried.

I hear you apologizing.

I hear you say you're sorry when your baby starts to cry just after the entrees are served and all you wanted was one nice dinner out. I hear you say you're sorry when your baby spits up on your visitor's dry-clean-only cashmere sweater. I hear you say you're sorry when you accidentally bump your baby. When you're warming up the bottle but it's still going to be three more minutes and you know she's hungry. When you have to wrap up dinner to relieve the babysitter. When you have to leave the meeting early because you have to pick up your child. When you're the last one at day care to pick up your child even though you left early. When you have to cancel plans because your baby is still sleeping. When you have to miss another day of work because that cough WAS something to worry about.

I hear you say you're sorry when you're just not ready for sex because your body is a milk-producing, saggy, sore, stretched out machine that is just so bloody tired in every inch of its miraculous, disastrous glory.

I hear you.

I hear you crying because of the hormones. I hear you crying because you can't stop throwing up. I hear you crying because you can't remember the last time you got two consecutive hours of sleep. I hear you crying because you miss your baby and you're back at work and you just weren't ready. I hear you crying because you got your period again. I hear you crying because your friend just announced that she's pregnant, and you want to be happy for her, but it's so hard. I hear you crying because you honestly don't know what you're doing and it physically hurts in your heart of hearts when you baby won't stop crying.

I hear you crying because it's so unexpectedly, excruciatingly hard to make a baby, carry a baby, grow a baby, keep a baby, birth a baby, feed a baby, soothe a baby, leave a baby, raise a baby.

I hear you telling her that she is the most beautiful thing in the world at 2am.

I hear you showing everyone the latest video of him in his bouncy chair.

I hear you listening to that first heartbeat on the ultrasound and telling yourself not to get too excited but screaming inside because maybe, just maybe, this is the beginning.

Motherhood is complex. It is learning biology, chemistry, physiology, psychology, and vocabulary that you never knew existed.

Motherhood is isolating, yet inclusive. It is understanding, yet judgmental. It is an overload of information, and yet completely without direction.

It is like sailing a sinking boat without a compass, and wondering at the beauty of the stars.

Mama - I hear you, I see you, I am you, and I am here for you.

You deserve love, you deserve patience, you deserve space, you deserve recognition. Because what you are going through every single day is unimaginably hard.

And you are doing the best job you possibly can.

The Fourth Trimester - After "Not Waving but Drowning"

Nobody heard her, the mother
But still she lay moaning:
She was caught in the current, a newborn,
And not waving but drowning.

Poor girl, she always loved babies,
And now she's birthed one
"It must be too much for her,"
They mumble.

Oh, no no no, it was too much always,
(She's crying while laundry is humming),
"I was much too far out, holding this little life,
And not waving but drowning."

Sunflower – A Poem for PPD

When life becomes heavy,
Too heavy for one,
I bend like a flower
That seeks out the sun.

My shoulders hunch forward
To carry the load,
I've lost several inches
Now that they are bowed.

My head brims with burdens,
The weight is immense,
I'm fractured and worried,
And nothing makes sense.

My body grows stronger,
It leans with the wind.
I know that I'll weather
This storm that I'm in.

But before this one passes,
It's you little one,
I'm the sunflower,
And you
Are my
Sun.

Moo

Maybe I wouldn't feel quite so defeated
If only my milk supply weren't so depleted.

Mechanical pumping repeats in my dreams,
I'm practically bovine, just churning out cream.

The washing, the pumping, the washing again,
The lactation experts who've now become friends.

The counting of ounces, the clearing of ducts—
I'm constantly starving. My diet is fucked.

First mastitis, sleeplessness, oversupply,
I dress to unbutton, 'cause why even try?

My freezer is bursting with bags that I've pumped.
I got a bit tipsy, now I'll have to dump.

Then plummeting, vanishing, where did it go?
I went back to work, and it screwed up my flow.

The wrestling of baby, the latching, the pain,
Who said this was natural? They must be insane.

Girl Friends

Here's to the girl friends
Who tell us it's hard,
Who show up postpartum
With more than a card.

Who answer our questions
We text late at night,
Who call us to see
If we're feeling alright.

Here's to the girl friends
We can't live without,
Who tell us "you're great"
When we're filled with self doubt.

Girl, thank you for being
My rock when I'm blue,
My life would sure suck
If I didn't have you.

M is for Mother

M is for mother.
Mom. Mommy. Mama. Mum.
Mine.
My memories melting
Into myriad monikers.

I multiplied. I made minis.

Watched them metastasize
From microscopic minnows,
Into magnetic marsupials
That mewed for milk.

I manufacture miracles,
Measure my day in moments,
Meditating on my methodology.

I moderate. Mollify. Mitigate
Mass mutiny.
I move, move, move.
I make mistakes.

I misplace myself, marvel
At the magnificence.
I am more

Than Mom.
I matter.

For My Friends

Lately I've been feeling,
A bit, well, out of sorts.
I'm tough to get a hold of,
And my free time's rather short.

Forgive me if I cancel,
Or miss a girls' night out,
It's hard to take the time away
When children are about.

I can't go get my nails done
'Cause my baby's daycare called -
He spiked a fever once again,
I can't go out at all.

I promise that I miss you,
And our friendship didn't stop,
Of all these balls I'm juggling
It's this one that I've dropped.

I know I'm acting distant,
See, things have changed a bit.
It's just my babies need me too,
I'm afraid I can't commit.

So thank you for your patience
As I find my feet again.
I'd love for you to come on by…
I really need my friend.

Sleep

Wake Up

I'm sorry that I woke you, Mom,
I know you need the sleep,
These emotions overwhelmed me,
And I may have made a peep.

I startled in the darkness,
And I couldn't see you there.
I needed arms around me,
I felt cold, alone, and scared.

Just rock me for a minute, Mom,
And kiss my sleepy head,
I'll snuggle on your shoulder,
Then I'll let you go to bed.

I won't always need you, Mom,
But tonight I hope you'll stay,
Rub my back and whisper
That you're here,
And it's ok.

You'll Never Sleep Again

"You'll never sleep again!" I heard
The other parents claim.
But now that I'm a mom, I think
That this should be reframed.

You'll wake when baby coughs or coos,
You'll wake when toddler screams,
You'll rouse to clean up accidents.
You'll rise to cure bad dreams.

It's not that you will never sleep,
Once "Mom" becomes your name.
It's that you'll keep an open ear -
You'll never sleep the same.

Sleep

In the midst of my 20's,
I was all doubt and fear.
Would I marry? Succeed?
Have a kick-ass career?

Now in my 30's,
Contentment comes cheap…

I'm mostly concerned
With the next time I'll sleep.

Bedtime Lullaby

Hang a star above your cradle,
Paint a moonbeam on your bed,
When you close your eyes, a galaxy
Will form within your head.

Swing just below the crescent
Of the moon up in the sky,
You can try to kick the stardust
When you pump your legs and fly.

Close your heavy eyelids, now,
I'll rock you like the sea,
We'll sail right off to dreamland,
Feel the wind, and breathe with me.

There are lanterns all around us,
They're reflected in the deep,
Imagine that you're floating, too,
And slowly drift
Asleep.

Nocturne Lullaby

It's past your bed time, little one.
Rest your head time, little one.
The eve is creeping, farewell sun.
It's time for sleeping, day is done.

The stars are winking in the sky.
Still your thinking, close your eyes.
Drift to dreamland, little one.
It's you and me, and, night's begun.

Listen darling, I am near.
Nothing's frightening, Mama's here.
Moon is calling, you must go.
Night is falling,
I love
You
So.

Bookends and Bedtales

I brought you a bedtale
I found on the shelf,
Between bookends and bobbles
And one little self.

One little self
That's tucked in all tight,
With a chin blanket blocking
The chill of the night.

When the chill of the night
Is the snow in the air,
And your breath comes in puffs
That pillow and flare.

They pillow and flare
With the nine o' clock chime,
And you're nodding and knotting
Your mind up in rhyme.

With your mind up in rhyme,
And your eyes down in bed,
You're drifting and sifting
Through sand in your head.

Through sand in your head,
We head for the hush,
And your cherubim cheeks
Grow rosy and flushed.

And rosy they grow,
As I help you count sheep,
And you star-slipping fall
Into dreams, into asleep.

Longer

I want to linger a little longer
For you'll grow bigger,
My love grow stronger.
I'll rock you slowly,
Against my shoulder,
A baby only 'till you get older.
This moment, darling,
Is ours alone.
I'll hold you closely,
This is your home.

The Early Years

Time is a Thief

Time is a thief
Who appears overnight,
To age all our children,
Somehow in plain sight.

I've been robbed of the months
And the days and the years,
I'm left putting clothes away,
Holding back tears.

Yes, time is a thief,
No one saw when he came,
He's stolen my babies…
I'm rich, all the same.

Cold Season

The seasons change, I know it's true:
It's now the time of cold and flu.
One week healthy, next week not.
Always guessing what they've caught.

Had a play date with a friend...
Spiked a fever, yet again.
Tell me, how can tiny tots
Produce that sheer amount of snot?

The PTO we have to take...
This "time off" is not a break.
Will this season ever end?
"Hi! It's daycare. Yes, again."

The Good Old Days

These are the days we'll remember,
The chaos, the tears, and the play,
The Saturday pancakes, the dinner time dancing,
The stories to close out the day.

These are the days we'll remember,
The nights when they climbed in our bed,
The bubble bath splashing, the rocks in their pockets,
The feel of a feverish head.

These are the days we'll remember,
The abandon of summer spent wild,
The echo of laughter, the weight on a shoulder
Of a sleepy and rosy-cheeked child.

These are the days we'll remember,
When we steal a quick squeeze or a kiss,
These are the moments to treasure -
Looking back,
They will be
Days we miss.

This Mess

Let them get dirty
And splash in a puddle,
Even if cleaning that stain
Is a struggle.

Let them throw noodles
And food on the floor
Don't wipe down their face yet,
Just help them explore.

Let them be little,
You'll get through somehow,
There's a lifetime to clean,
But they're children
Right now.

In Her Shoes

Sometimes I miss her.
She was wild as the ocean,
And flew across many.
She wore three-inch, platform heels,
Trailing confidence.
She ran departments, teams,
Initiatives, races.
She GOT SHIT DONE.
She drank fancy cocktails
Until wee hours,
Gathering stories in her purse,
And people in her arms.

I catch her
In sidelong, furtive, mirror glances.
Beneath the dark circles,
And the new wrinkles,
She winks and whispers,
"You are you,
You're still you."
I see her
In my daughter teetering
To stand in her mother's heels,
Trying to walk in my shoes.

Remember

You're brave, my love, and brilliant, too.
No mountain is too high for you.
You're stronger than you can believe,
There is no goal you can't achieve.
I'm here to help you learn and grow -
I love you more
Than you can know.

Standoff

As a parent you choose
All the battles to fight.
Wear your ballgown this morning?
Well, I guess that's alright.

We're hosting a party…
So, screen time tonight!
But, don't pee on the sidewalk,
That's just not polite.

Parenting teaches us
What will be fine,
When we're constantly changing
Where we draw the line.

In the end, all our boundaries
Are just asinine,
'Cause children will triumph
Eight times out of nine.

Laundry

In new parent classes
Why don't they disclose
How much time in your life
Will be spent washing clothes?

The volume of laundry
I tackle each week
Does not seem to jive with
My children's physique.

The washing, the drying,
The folding I do
Is a wormhole I'm certain
All parents go through.

(I know I'm complaining,
And I shouldn't pout,
I'm sure that I'll miss it
When they one day move out),

If I teach my young toddler
To wash what I've asked her,

Does that make me genius…
Or just a slave master?

Recital

Side to side, head to chest,
Softly arching arabesque.

Faintly falling into line,
Dainty darlings, so refined/

Feet wrapped up in silken bows,
Pink and perfect, head to toe.

Tulle is twirling, hands outstretched—
Softly arching arabesque.

Gently treading, toes on floor,
Bodies threading heart to core.

Limbs that wobble, now hold strong,
Barely muscled, lean and long.

Eyes are focused for the test—
Softly arching arabesque.

Small leaves swirling in a stream,
Pulled by current here unseen.

Lose themselves in the music's flow—
Dainty darlings, fresh as snow.

Crescendo builds, and then they rest,
Each one hoping she was best.

Who was watching daughter blessed
Perform the perfect arabesque?

On Your First Day of School

You stand a bit taller,
Each step that you take,
There's a tug on my heartstrings,
Inside, there's an ache.

You've filled up your backpack
With pencils and dreams,
My head brims with worry,
I burst at the seams.

Will you bond with your teacher?
Will you make many friends?
Will you trust me with stories
When each school day ends?

Today may be hard, but
I promise, we'll grow.
Each day brings a lesson
That we need to know.

I love you, my darling,
I hope that it shows.
As you start this adventure,
I am here,
Letting go.

Affirmations

I hope that you love food,
And eat what you wish,
But I'll never force you
To finish a dish.

When you go to the doctor
And must get a shot,
You can say "ouch!" or crumple -
'Cause shots hurt a lot.

It's ok in some moments
To not be ok.
No life is all sunshine,
We live in the grey.

I won't tell you "Be careful,"
When you go explore,
I may tell you "Good job!", but
Please praise yourself more.

You owe hugs to no one.
You don't need to smile.
Some days will be marathons.
Some years are miles.

These affirmations
Will always be true.
You are loved.

You are valued.
You are perfect
As you.

Mom Guilt

Apology

Can I talk to you, baby?
I know you're upset.
Mama wants to say sorry
For some things I regret.

You see, Mama is human,
And I made a mistake.
When I'm feeling frustration,
My patience can break.

I know you're still little,
With so much to learn,
Like sharing with others
And waiting your turn.

My anger seems scary—
You're doing your best.
Please try to forgive me
For failing this test.

You're a good kid, my darling,
I'm not mad at you.
It's these moments we'll work on.
I'm still learning, too.

So baby, I'm sorry.
Please know that I care.
We'll get through this together.

Let's try to repair.
I'll love you forever.
I'll always be there.

Here

"No, no! Please don't go!
I'll eat you up, I love you so!"
Your favorite book, as stories go,
You shout "again!"
I tell you, "no…

It's bedtime, love, we've had our fun.
I'll sing a song, but only one."
Your little hands reach round my head
And hold on tight as you fight bed.

"Mama can you play with me?"
You've set out plates
And cups for tea.
"In a minute, then I'll come,
I have to get this one thing done."

I pack your lunch. I clear the sink.
I brew a coffee I won't drink.
I make a call. It's time to leave.
There's no more time
For make believe.

Then after school, I'm on my phone,
I tell you "Please, just play alone!

I have to get this email out."
Your eyes well up. You stomp and pout.

A busy mom I've been all day…
Putting toys and clothes away,
Running errands, working too,
No time for play, less time for you.

Just once perhaps I'll leave the plates.
I'll read the book. You'll stay up late.
I can't stop time, but it can slow.
I'm here with you.
I will not go.

It's been a DAY

Today has been a challenge,
And I'm feeling more than spent.
I wish that I could find the words
To capture how it went.

The children woke up early,
My ambitions still were high -
A family outing somewhere fun!
No one would shout or cry.

Then, soon it all went sideways,
When at last we'd packed the car.
The toddler had an accident
Before we could get far.

We rerouted to a playground,
Where the baby threw a fit.
I thought I'd packed the paci,
But…there was no sign of it.

The toddler scraped her knee cap,
Then the baby's diaper leaked,
We had a testy, spiteful fight,
Before the sun had peaked.

Then no one wanted dinner.
I stained my favorite shirt.
The baby bit my thigh. I cussed.
'Cause yeah, it fucking hurt.

Their bedtime took forever,
But I tried to be a mom.
I couldn't help but check the clock,
As story time dragged on.

Some days like this can break me,
When it's rough right from the start.

But then they say,
"I love you, mom."
And mend
My broken heart.

Sorry

To my children:
I'm sorry that I yelled at you,
I'm sorry that I snapped,
I'm sorry that I couldn't look
When you said "Look at that!"
I'm sorry that I'm tired
When you ask me if I'll play,
I'm sorry that I failed the test
Of parenting today.

To my husband:
I'm sorry that I don't want sex
Or dress up very much,
I'm sorry that I snapped at YOU,
And don't want to be touched.

To my friends and family:
I'm sorry that I haven't called,
I hope you're doing fine.
I'm drowning here in parenting,
But know you're on my mind.

To myself:
I'm sorry that I don't make time
To treat my body right.

I don't work out, or feed you greens,
Or let you sleep at night.

I'm filled with such apologies,
There's always too much stuff.
There's simply not a perfect me,
I hope that I'm enough.

What do you Do?

"What do you do?" is a question I hate.
Because "Stay at home mom"
Doesn't quite take the cake.

I manage life cycles of projects en masse,
Initiate planning and daily forecasts,
Oversee budgets, and manage a team,
Engage outside experts both up and downstream.

I'd love to hear more about work that you do,
After all, I once juggled a corporate life, too.

Here is my C.V., yep, I've done it all.
My skill set's expansive,
My team members, small.

Mom Math

Since I became "mom," it seems
I've gotten good at math,
I'm always calculating things,
Like time for meals and baths,

I add up all the diapers, and
Subtract remaining snacks,
I divide the day in hours, then
I plan what should be packed.

I've never been a fan of math,
I'm right-brained by persuasion,
I guess I never factored in
Some kids to that equation.

Partnership

Sex and Marriage

A wild night in our twenties
Was staying out late.
And now in our thirties,
It's "kids down by eight!"

You want to seduce me?
Nix restaurants and wine.
I just want a good dose
Of some solid "me time."

You know what I find
More romantic than flowers?
Don't ask me a question
For 24 hours.

No whining. No pulling.
No crying. No "Please!"
No feeding. No laundry.
Just sweet, blissful peace.

Before I can get
Down and dirty with you…
I need to remember
How to love myself, too.

You

We were young when we first met.
Now we have kids, we may forget
Those hours spent within the thrall
Of early love, but I recall
The trips we took, the dates we had,
Those silly fights that weren't so bad.

Now I'm a mom, and you're a dad.

Our bodies may not be the same,
But look at what our life became!
Those people that we were before
Could never guess what lay in store.
And though I may not tell you so,
I hope my feelings will still show.

I'm proud to watch our family grow.

Some days, when we are short on rest,
Our patience may not be the best.
Occasionally, you're cross and shout.
At times I'll snap. We'll work it out.
We've learned to let the small things slide,
And know our lives change like the tide.

I'm better when you're by my side.

I know we're buys every day,
And sometimes don't make time to say,
"Thanks." "You're hote." Or even kiss.
I guess that's why I've written this.
With everything that we've bene through,
I want to tell you what holds true:

Now you're a dad, our life feels new.
I'm falling more in love with you.

Invisible Woman

In family photos, you will see
Children smiling, wild and free.

Their father playing in the sand,
A tender moment, toys in hand.

Behind the camera, I was near,
But often seem to disappear.

Then once at home when things are calm,
I search our pics for "Proof of Mom."

Our family's four, it isn't three.
But who takes pictures?
Yeah, that's me.

Mama Needs a Minute

Mama needs a minute.
Oof, I am really in it.
Can you please just let me finish?
Mama needs a minute.

Mama hasn't eaten,
Her body's feeling beaten,
Her coffee's close to freezing,
From all this family pleasing.

Did mama pack the lunches?
She's rolling with the punches
Mama needs a minute,
(But it's a sin when she commits it).

Where is your newest jacket,
Your hat, did mama pack it?
Your juice, did brother spill it?
Here, let mama fill it.

Mama's friend is talking,
But baby needs some rocking...
Can't muster concentration
To engage in conversation.

Mama turned the laundry. Mama washed a pan.
Mama fed the children. Mama washed their hands.
Mama packed their school bags. Mama brushed their hair.

Mama tucked them in at night and woke when they were
scared.
Mama booked appointments for the dentist and the doc.
Mama made a grocery list and ordered from the shop.
Mama fed the kitty. Mama walked the dog.
Mama booked speech therapy, then cried in the garage.

Mama folded laundry and put it all away.
Daddy pats her ass and asks,
"And what'd you do today?"

"Mama needs a minute,
I'm failing, can I quit it?"

He rubs my shoulders, takes a breath.
Then holds me close and says "go rest.
You're doing great, a brilliant mom.
We're in it now, but things will calm.
Take a minute, hell take two.
I've got the kids,
and I've got you."

Light Bites

Gym

I'm sorry, we're done.
It's over. We're through.

Let's be realistic,
It's not me, it's you.
I know we both tried,
But I still have my doubts…

This relationship, gym,
Just will not
Work out.

Couple Goals

I'm glad that I'm with you,
You're not a complainer.

And you still find me sexy
When I wear
My retainer.

Fridays – a Haiku

The kids are asleep.
Let's Netflix and talk about
When we still had sex.

Crunchy

I tried to be a crunchy mom,
I was one in my head.
Glass bottles, diapers made of cloth,
My own purees instead.

I quickly learned that that's not me,
I'm just not built that way.
I barely keep my kids alive…
I'll save the earth
Another day.

The League

It happens every year, come Fall,
I see my husband…not at all.

I know I'll have him back again
When football season's at an end.

A Sunday that he spends with me?
That's my only "fantasy."

Tupperware

The most frustrating thing
Of which I'm aware,

Is locating which lid
Goes with what Tupperware.

Mondays

Mondays are blue,
Roses are red.

If we talk before coffee,
I'll bite off your head.

Target

I need bath soap, and tampons,
And towels, and garlic…
A reasonable person
Would go to the market.

Three hours later…
I've bought half of Target.

Postpartum Fitness

6 a.m. on a trail
Is where you'll never find me.

I could not run a mile
If a bear were behind me.

Mom-Petition

As a mother, I find some hilarity
In our community's quest to find parity.

On Insta, you'll never see clarity,
'cause perfection is all that they share-ity.

The truth is, (I'm serious, bare with me),
Honesty's really a rarity.

About the Author

Anne Marie Brown is a lyrical poet, children's book author, and mother to two little ones, Malia and Jack.

She majored in Creative Writing, Poetry at Colorado College, and holds an MBA from the Darden School of Business, University of Virginia.

She is represented by the Andrea Brown Literary Agency. She resides in Denver, Colorado, where she and her husband, Matt, spend their time chasing after their kids, hiking, and skiing.

Her poetry can be found on

Instagram: @BrunchPoet
and
Tik Tok: @AMBrownAuthor

Made in the USA
Monee, IL
09 January 2022